The Birth Of Parsival

*

THE BIRTH OF PARSIVAL

BY THE SAME AUTHOR

CECILIA GONZAGA

A DRAMA

Fcp. 8vo, 2s. 6d. net

LONGMANS, GREEN, AND CO.
LONDON, NEW YORK, AND BOMBAY

THE

BIRTH OF PARSIVAL

BY

R. C. TREVELYAN

AUTHOR OF "CECILIA GONZAGA"
AND "POLYPHEMUS AND OTHER POEMS"

LONGMANS, GREEN, AND CO.

39 PATERNOSTER ROW, LONDON

NEW YORK AND BOMBAY

1905

TO

B. A. W. R.

THE ARGUMENT

Titurel, lord of Monsalvat, Keeper of the
Grail and Lance, the holy symbols of Christ's
passion, fallen upon sickness and old age, by command of Kundry the prophetess, delivered over
his sacred office to Frimutel his son, born to him
in such chaste wedlock as is lawful to the king
alone of all that consecrated knighthood.   Therewith he omitted not to instruct his heir in all the
mysteries of the Grail, and most earnestly to
forewarn him that to none, no, not even to the
king himself, are the delights of love permitted,
except it shall thus have been expressly and in
due season appointed by the Grail's divine oracle,
that so for that high service there might never
fail a pure and noble race.   Nevertheless this
Frimutel, though for a while he transgressed not
this covenant of his heritage, yet at length in the
hour of temptation, being tried and found wanting,

fell. For, after by his sole wisdom and valour he had delivered from a great host of heathen enemies a far-distant kingdom whither he had been sent at the bidding of the Grail, Love, that with ease can vanquish even the most mighty conquerors, laid wait for him in the eyes of Herzeloida, the virgin daughter of the king, and thence entered into his heart with such sudden and tyrannous force, that he forthwith despised and set at nought, or rather utterly forgot, what he should then most have remembered, and so in secret brought to pass both her ruin and his own. For now the Grail, that seeth in secret, sent forth Kundry, its faithful minister, upon a grievous errand, whereof as yet she knows not the full cause, who coming by night where for a second time the sword of Frimutel had that same day vanquished the pagan hosts in a consummating overthrow, and with her own eyes beholding his apostacy, denounced against him the doom of dethronement, and madness, and immeasurable woe. Yet not so could the pride of Frimutel be subdued, but, magnanimous and unrepentant still, he drew forth the magic sword of the Grail, and defiantly, indignantly breaking it in sunder, imprecated a devastating curse upon any man who thereafter should make it whole. Little did he then foresee how upon his own son Parsival that curse should one day alight. But meanwhile in himself already was the swift vengeance of Heaven made manifest; for now, mastered by extravagant delusions, he entered the tent of the king's two sons and slew them while they slept; after which deed he was driven forth by his frenzy into the uninhabited solitudes of the forest, where for a whole year, more like a savage beast than a man, he dwelt alone amid the obscure shadows of his own violent and lawless thoughts.

Meantime in due course a son was born to the princess Herzeloida, and awhile, through the care of her faithful women, and the humane wisdom of Kundry, the truth was kept concealed. Yet not long afterwards was she compelled by strange and unforeseen fortune to make confession of her shame before her father, who thereupon, moved by a too hasty indignation, and prompted by the intolerant malice of the priest Thaddæus, her enemy, commanded her to be exposed, together with her infant, to the uncertain mercy of chance in some wild and remote region of the forest. Here then did Frimutel find them, and forthwith at the sight of her misery his madness departed from him, but not therewith his overweening and rebellious thoughts. In vain did she plead with him earnestly to repent; and at last, despite her great love for him, despite his most passionate supplication that she should not now forsake him, heavy at heart she departed with Kundry, who had come thither to lead her to that place appointed by the Grail, where she might bring up her son Parsival in holiness and peace, until the day when he should be required of her again.

ACT I

*A camp in a moonlit valley surrounded by low hills.
In the foreground to the left, overhung by boughs
of oak-trees, apart from the other tents, stands
one smaller than the rest, reserved for* FRIMUTEL
*alone. Some distance beyond is a large tent,
beautifully embroidered, where the king's sons are
sleeping. In the background many tents are seen
indistinctly gleaming in the moonlight, among
groups of tall trees here and there.*

KUNDRY *enters slowly from the right, and pauses in
front of* FRIMUTEL'S *tent. She is tall of stature,
and her aspect is aged yet still vigorous, like that
of an antique Sibyl. She stands for a while as
though lost in thought, then lifts her head and
speaks in a low tone.*

KUNDRY

Here hath my bitter journey reached an end :
The morrow's woe here now must I abide.
O chaste and holy Night, and you, ye Stars,

Ye ancient, deathless dynasties of heaven,
Who, steadfast in your ordered courses, serve
Your Maker's will, rebuking so vain man's
Proud, lawless thoughts, and thou, compassionate
    Moon,
To thee too would I call !—regard my misery !
Behold with what abhorrence and remorse
To my reluctant task constrained I come !
Oh bear me witness, when on Frimutel
Heaven's doom of shame, dethronement and dis-
    aster
By me denounced shall fall, nought but the
    Grail's
Divine commandment only could compel
My lips to curse this consecrated head,
Christ's own anointed king, His chosen champion !
Let me not know the cause, O righteous God !
Let me not know the cause!   If 'tis Thy will,
If this indeed must be, oh then withhold
At least all knowledge from me what transgres-
    sion
Could thus provoke Thy wrath, for what foul
    sin
Thou hast rejected whom Thou so didst love.
In blind submissive faith let me perform
This task, lest zeal's excess make hard my heart,

And parch the springs of human pity there.
That Thou hast judged him, me let that suffice.

> [*She withdraws slowly towards the right,
> until in the shadow of a tree her form
> can no longer be distinguished.*
>
> *The Curtain of* FRIMUTEL's *tent is opened
> from within, and he comes out.* HERZE-
> LOIDA *is seen standing in the entrance of
> the tent behind him.   He speaks in a quiet
> voice, looking away from her into the night.*

FRIMUTEL

Urge me no more. My name thou mayst not
  know.
Thrust from thy mind these bootless questioning
  thoughts.
They can but vainly mar Love's own serene
And trustful hour.   Rather stand by me here ;
Let us look forth into the tranquil night.
All things are silent round us : horse and man,
Tired with victorious battle, slumber sound :
Upon the silken tents the moonlight dreams :
No least breath stirs : it is so very still,
The night itself seems now as though it slept.
Alone within our hearts, love sleeps not there.

3

HERZELOIDA (*coming forward*)

Thou shalt not foil me thus : nay, dear lord,
Not all the tender cunning Loye's tongue knows
Shall serve thee now to baffle my heart's search,
Or charm to sleep the question striving there.
Reveal thy name : tell who thou art, and whence.
Is it not but an easy, slight return
I ask thee, I who have yielded to thee all
That thou couldst ask, yea, all was mine to give ?

FRIMUTEL

Herzeloida !

HERZELOIDA

How sweet upon thy lips doth sound my name !
Oh, why not thine on mine ? Nay, that poor
    boon,
After so many kisses they have given,
Is surely now their due. Then grudge them
    not.
Beasts of the field love and part nameless thus.
Her lover's name is to a woman's heart
Dear as their native speech to men long banished.
Ah me, what aching doubts thy silence breeds !
What if thou shouldst grow weary of thy love.
So surely shall it wane, as wanes even now

This night's brief beauty into bitter dawn.
Unknown from the unknown didst thou come
    forth,   .
And thither shalt return, my heart portends.

FRIMUTEL

Never will I forsake thee : doubt not that.
Even now already art thou not my bride,
As Love in secret knows ?   Have I not sworn
To-morrow from thy sire to claim thy hand ?
Then put such blind fears from thee.   On thy lips,
Here is my glory's harbour, my hope's port.
A noble recompense thy love shall be
For all, to win thy love, I have forgone.
Yet not mean nor inglorious deem my state.
Among earth's kings no lot more proud than mine.

HERZELOIDA

If verily so glorious was thy fate,
How long ingloriously wilt thou endure
Here to consume thy days ?   Soon in thy heart
Restless remembrance shall awake of deeds
Done proudly long ago and greatness gone :
Thy nobler destinies shall call thee hence,
And thou wilt surely some day leave me here,

Forlorn, and widowed even of thy name,
Without so much as that fond solace left
To haunt as with some hope-starved ghost of joy
My lost days crawling deathward with their shame.
Oh let me know thy name : so shall my trust
Be wholly thine, as my heart's love already.

FRIMUTEL

Is then thy faith so frail ?   Seem I indeed
To thee so worthless of thy trust, so base ?
Hear then who once I was, yet am no more,
Since for thy love's sake have I cast away
My name, my honour too.
Titurel was my sire.   While yet the Grail,
By him committed to these hands, was mine,
Frimutel was I called.

HERZELOIDA

Art thou indeed son to that Titurel,
Of whom men tell how to his sinless hands,
Alone found worthy such high charge, the Grail
By Heaven was given ?   Oh, if his son thou art,
Then woe to thee, unhappy Frimutel !
And woe to me, most wretched among women !
Into what sin for my sake art thou fallen !

6

FRIMUTEL

Let not this knowledge so dismay your heart.
Give it glad welcome rather, since therefrom
Thou now mayst know the measure of my love
Which for thy love's sake hath so greatly dared.
My name thou now hast heard, and whence I come.
That thither I return not, that know too.
While last our lives, so long shall last our loves.

HERZELOIDA

Ah, Frimutel, how may that be, alas !
Let those boast thus who love yet still are wise,
Whose love ne'er made them sin, as ours has done.
Such joy as ours has been lasts but a season :
Repentance is its heir, or shame and death.
For thee indeed, doubt not, it must be so :
Oh then repent : yet, ere it be too late,
Cast sinful love away : repent and live.
For me, so Heaven's vengeance for our sin
Fall not upon thy head, what care I now
Though as love's season brief my life should be ?

FRIMUTEL

Let us bear souls too noble for such fears.
Never need mine repent, or thine despair.

7

One master, but no more, the mind can serve :
And passion, not repentance, yet rules ours.
Is Love our lord, then while Love reigneth, lords
Of Life are we, not Sin's abjected thralls.
What room is here then for repentance ?   Nay,
Though Heaven threat vengeance o'er us, in our sin
Masterful Love would have us glory still :—
If sin indeed it be ;—since who condemns us ?
Reason condemns not Love : and shall God's curse
Forbid what Reason hath sanctified and blest ?
Lift up thine eyes : consider yonder stars :
From everlasting to everlasting they,
Pale bondsmen to Necessity, perform
The unalterable ordinance of God's will,
Yet know they nought thereof, nor of their toil
Grow weary, nor therein find joy at all,
Without death, without passion, without will,
And without Love.   Therefore the mind of man
Is of an essence nobler than these are.
He too serves God no less, but freely serves,
Of his own will, knowing that God is good,
Who to know good from evil gave him power
By divine Reason, of His gifts the noblest.
Then let not blind tradition daunt our souls :
But, wouldst thou know what God would have
      us do,

Rather give ear to Reason, whose clear voice
Bids us make much of life, while yet we may,
Redeeming and enhancing with some joy,
Some brightness from Love's face, time's weary waste
Of barren hours : so may we serve Him best.

HERZELOIDA

Fain would I so believe as thou wouldst have me.

FRIMUTEL

Dare only to believe ; once dare, already
Thy doubts shall be illumined and dispersed.

HERZELOIDA

Ah yet too well I know that we have sinned ;
And to my conscience would I still be true.
So thine thou wrong not, all may yet be well.
When late or soon as from a pleasing dream's
Vain flattering assurance thou shalt wake,
When Reason, whom thou hast trusted as thy
        friend,
Becomes thy judge, oh then may pride and shame,
Too scornful of itself, not tempt thy soul
Still to reject repentance and that mercy
Which from the contrite heart God ne'er withholds.

FRIMUTEL

It is not I that dream ; nay, 'tis thyself
Whom these vain apprehensions daunt.   Let those
Repent, who wilfully against heaven's light
Have sinned, not I, who inwardly by truth's
Clear dawn illumined, thus have dared cast off
The bonds of superstition and base fear.

HERZELOIDA

Ah Frimutel, the thoughts of man are dark
As darkness' self : to search and know them, none
That lives hath power, no, not the soul wherein
In secret they were formed.   Yet God, to whom
The darkness and the light are both alike,
Searcheth and trieth all : no thought so swift
But when new-born it issues from the soul
Furtively without sound, without a name,
That very instant is it known and judged,
If it be pure, approved, or if perverse,
Condemned.   Oh then beware lest thou mistake
The o'erweening promptings of thine own proud
    heart
For God's authentic voice.   Yet none the less,
While life endures, thine will I be ; on both,
By love and sin united and made one,
If so 'tis destined, let one judgment fall.

FRIMUTEL

How noble is thy heart even in its error,
As this thy longing shows with me to share
Vainly feared penance for imagined sin.
But good only, not evil, is in our choice,
So we have faith, to share.

                          But see, the moon
Behind yon trees is setting, and new light
Begins to wash the fading stars with grey.
Thou shouldst begone : 'tis danger for thee now
Here to stay with me.   Then, sweet love, farewell !

HERZELOIDA

Farewell !   As I thy heart, so thou hast mine.
    [*She goes out to the left.*
      FRIMUTEL *remains standing before the tent,*
         as though tranced in thought.   At length
         he speaks.

FRIMUTEL

Dark are the thoughts of man : so said she truly.
Aye, dark indeed as very darkness' self.
And yet where else is light ?
Where else save in the soul ?   Or if not there,

Then have we no communion with the light,
Nor yet with God, whose essence is the light.
Or else God is not anywhere at all,
And we children of darkness, and not light.
To entertain such doubt, that were impiety,
Worse than my error, if indeed I err.
From God, from God this impulse came, I know,
That taught me thus by Love's might to deliver
The Grail, the holy symbol of His Love,
Champion and lord whereof He hath ordained me,
From ignoble superstition,
From joyless and loveless worship,
Ignorant and irrational and vain.
                 (*A pause*)
Nay, to what end thus plead I with my soul?
Why do I heap up words,
Unprofitable words,
Since, though I boast, my striving thoughts
Are not appeased?
Words cannot make truth, no, nor silence doubt:
Though therefore the more confident and strong
Through the still chambers of the heart they
      sound,
Yet, when they cease, doubt's voice still whispers
      there.
If I have sinned,

Why boast I thus my innocence in vain?
Shall man contend with God, or reason with
    Him?
According to His wisdom shall He judge,
And none, until His justice be revealed,
Hath knowledge of His law. Nay, what man
    knoweth
If any law or judge there be at all?
Best then endure, be what it may, the end.
When that must come, then will it come: yet
    me
No coward shall it find; since not unrighteous,
Even though God condemn, to my own soul
Still must I seem—Then welcome, Death!
If Love indeed be sin, sin's wages Death,
Why should I fear thee? Where is now thy
    sting?

     [*He remains gazing before him. The day
       begins to break, and each minute it grows
       more light.*

      KUNDRY *approaches from the right, and
       standing a little distance behind* FRIMU-
      TEL, *speaks in a low voice.*

KUNDRY

Frimutel!

13

FRIMUTEL

(Lifting his head, but without turning, answers
as in a trance)

Who art thou that callest me by name?
    [KUNDRY, *coming nearer, and standing beside*
      FRIMUTEL, *speaks again quietly.*

KUNDRY

Frimutel, I am Kundry.
Well dost thou know me: from the Grail am I
    come.
What dost thou here, Frimutel?

FRIMUTEL *(still without turning his head)*

Hail to thee, Kundry!
So soon then art thou come,
Through forest and over mountain sped by the
    Grail from afar
Hither to greet its king
By the might of its holy sword victor in
    battle?
Nay, for a victory nobler and mightier far

I doubt not but thou from the Grail hast come to
    hail me.
For more than the host of my foes
Have I vanquished this day ;
I have made strong my soul, I have cast
Vain fear for ever from me ;
The priest's dark curse have I scorned,
The threats of his jealous pride :
I have won for my bed a bride, a queen for the
    throne of the Grail.
For man's law changeth and passeth
Away with his breath :
But the law of love is perfect,
Divine, and stronger than death.
Then exult with me, Kundry ;
Let my joy be thine :
To the Knights of the Grail
Speed back with glad tidings :
Broken, for ever broken,
By Love's might broken forever be the bonds
Of tradition shameful and vain
On the Grail's heroic knighthood of old by priest-
    craft basely,
Falsely imposed, in ignorance or scorn
Of man's free noble nature and God's law.

KUNDRY

Oh, perishing soul !
Even yet on Hell's brink pause, pause and look
  back.
Repent, confess to Heaven thy sin, seek pardon.
Yet, even yet thou mayst.

FRIMUTEL

Is this thine errand, Kundry ?
To curse and not to bless me hast thou come ?
Nay then, bid me not pause.
Repent I cannot : ask not that of me.

KUNDRY

Ah, yet thou canst—yet, ere thy doom hath fallen.

FRIMUTEL

If it must fall, then quickly let it fall.
Already have I paused :
A voice more dear, more moving to my soul
Than thine hath pleaded with me, vainly pleaded.
Then think not thou to move me.

KUNDRY

Ah, woe, woe ! Shame and woe
To thy kingly house, O sinless Titurel !
Alas for thee, Monsalvat !
Shamed is thy throne, thy holy knighthood's law !
And misery, ah misery to thee,
Thou proud apostate spirit,
Once to thy sacred office and high charge
Ordained by Heaven ! How art thou fallen now !
Hear then thy doom : the Grail whose law in scorn
Thou hast rejected and transgressed, henceforth
Shall scorn and reject thee. Also thy reason,
Wherein too proudly glorying thou didst sin,
Shall now be taken from thee : on thy heart
Frenzy shall fall : forth from the face of man
Into the forest shalt thou go, with beasts
Less wild and fierce than thee to make thy lair.
Nevertheless, that thou mayst still repent,
At length thy reason after many days
Shall be restored thee, on that hour when first
Thine eyes, grown clear, shall look upon what woe
Thy sin hath wrought. But whether then remorse
Shall wake within thy heart, or yet more deep
Into the night of sin, past hope of grace,
Thy fate shall be to fall, I know not that :

Yet this last misery, of all thy doom
Most miserable, 'tis given me now to know :
That which from thy rebellion shall be born,
If thou destroy not, thee shall it destroy.
Such is thy sentence, O proud Frimutel !
Bitter for me, who pity thee, to speak,
And for thy soul hereafter to endure.

> [KUNDRY *turns to go.* *The tree tops are*
> *already filled with sunlight.*

FRIMUTEL

Stay, Kundry !

KUNDRY

What more wouldst thou with me, Frimutel ?

FRIMUTEL

Because I have not scorned
Reason, God's noblest gift to man, but still
In all things by its guidance sought for Truth ;
Because, by Truth enlightened,
The mysteries of Love I now have found
No sacrament of Satan vain and impious,
But by God's blessing sanctified and holy ;
Because I would not stoop my soul to worship
Despair's dark idols, false religion's dreams,

Ignorant envy's errors—therefore now,
Scorned, cursed and rejected of the Grail,
Its wrath with joy I welcome, and its curse
I scorn.   Nay, though the Grail renounce not me,
Yet such ignoble service willingly
Would courage and true noble worth abjure.
Since then between me and the Grail henceforth
No peace can be, as a foe's gift this sword
No longer will I trust nor deign to wear,
But whence 'twas given me now would render back.

> [*As he draws forth the sword, a ray of*
> *sunlight catches the blade.*

Farewell, thou noble sword !
For the last time within thy master's hand
Greet thou the glorious sun with thy bright laughter.
Worthily have I worn thee, loved thee well,
Nor ever found thee faithless at my need.
Nay then, proud sword,
Never let hand less mighty nor more base
Draw thee to my dishonour and thine own.
Terrible, strong and beautiful thou wert ;
No earthly cunning tempered thy fierce steel ;
Thy magic blade, enwrought with figured spells
And mystic script, no craft of man e'er shaped.
Doubtless upon the anvils of the stars
At God's command by angels wert thou forged,

And in the river of the water of life
That springs beneath His throne, there wast thou
    dipped,
That so thy beauty and strength, assured against
Destruction and decay, might never perish,
Nor ever cease to mock the strength of man,
And slay his beauty.   Yet thus, thou proud sword,
Thus do I break thee.

        [*He puts forth his strength and breaks
        the sword.*

◄ KUNDRY

O, horror, horror !   Misery and horror !
Ah me, what hast thou done !
What deed of sacrilege and woe most dire,
Thou impious, violent man !

FRIMUTEL

*(With growing exaltation, holding up the
fragments of the sword)*

How now, ye sorry master-smiths of Heaven !
Look hither and behold your handiwork,
These poor dishonoured remnants of sad steel !
Well may your Master chide his skill-less slaves.
Arms which celestial artifice hath wrought

And tempered for eternity, should man
To your disgrace thus lightly break in sunder?
Down, vile splinters, down to the ground I fling you;
Thus 'neath my foot spurn you. And who shall dare
To make that whole which I have broken? Nay,
If any be so bold, woe to that man!
To his own shame and sorrow may he wear thee:
That which is dearest to him mayst thou slay:
And though on earth I draw this breath no more,
Yet shall my curse, within thee living still,
Ruthlessly urge him on from deed to deed
Through shame and desolation to despair.
Now, Kundry, to Monsalvat haste thee back,
Bearing these relics hallowed by my curse,
And there relate what thou hast seen and heard.

> [KUNDRY *silently gathers the fragments of the*
> *sword from the ground, and departs.*
>
> FRIMUTEL *sits down beneath a tree towards*
> *the right of the stage. A storm is gather-*
> *ing in the East, darkening the sun. He*
> *speaks musingly.*

FRIMUTEL

If thou destroy it not,
Then thee shall it destroy!
Verily wise and righteous are Thy judgments,

O God of Abraham !
Him Thou didst tempt of old,
As now by such dire choice Thou wouldst tempt me.
Abraham feared Thy wrath, therefore withheld not
His only son whom his soul loved : but I,
For what cause should I fear Thee !
Death have I never feared.   What worse thereafter
Thy vengeance can inflict, I can endure.
(A pause)
If thou destroy it not,
Then thee shall it destroy !
Is that God's truth ?   Doth He indeed speak thus ?
Yet, if it be not He, who then is it ?
No !—Loth am I yet so to believe.
Let me have proof more sure.
How know I if this wild ill-omened witch
Spoke truth at all ?   What if to my destruction
Some lying spirit entering hath possessed
Her credulous soul with false prophetic fury ?
Doth then God suffer Satan thus to abuse
His holy Name to tempt me to my ruin ?
(A pause)
O that I knew where I might find Him !
O that I now might come before His throne !
Then would I justify my soul :
Then would I plead my cause and reason with Him.

If He were just, then would He not condemn me.
Nay, were He just, here would He come to seek me,
Here answer my complaint, and judge my cause.
If I have sinned, yet knew it not,
Wherefore did He not show me mine iniquity,
That mine eyes might be opened to behold
And know my fault, and own my sentence just?

But that now will I never.
Why should my lips deny my innocence?
Though He condemn my soul, why should I fear
    Him?
Though He oppress me, nay, though now His wrath
Smite me, not therefore will I call Him just.
      [Meanwhile the whole of the eastern sky has
           become darkened by the approaching storm.
           A sound of distant thunder is heard.
Ah, ha! What now! Hath at length
The voice of my defiance reached His throne?
Hath it broken His careless calm, and stung His pride,
That He rouseth Himself and thundereth from afar?
His face is veiled in blackness: across the sun
He spreadeth His clouds: His coming is like the
    night.
      [The thunder is heard again somewhat nearer.
      FRIMUTEL *starts to his feet.*

Ho ! There once more from afar the voice of His
  wrath !
Wherefore so doth He tarry ?
Feareth He then the shame of my reproach
Knowing Himself unjust ?
Or haply He doth but threaten,
And now passeth another way in scorn,
Having given His angels charge that I escape not,
Nor foil by flight the leisure of His revenge.
So it must be : for behold !
What tents are these ? Aye, doubtless
These are the hosts of His angels camped around me,
Descended on an instant at His word.
This way and that, far as the eye can reach,
The valley is filled, the slopes are covered with
  them.
Each in his station confident and secure
They keep their silent watch around their prey.
I have resolved the thing that I will do :
Stealthily will I enter yonder tent,
And, be he angel or archangel, none
Shall thence escape my hands. When I have slain
  them,
I will come forth, and beneath heaven vaunt
My deed aloud, and publish my defiance.
Then doubtless He will turn again in haste

Terribly to avenge His slaughtered slaves.
Thus like a triumph, nobly, my death shall come.

> [*He goes towards the tent of the* KING'S SONS,
> *and enters. After a few moments he
> reappears and returns slowly to the front
> of the stage.*

How calm they sleep ! 'Tis strange !
I had not thought to find them sleeping so.
I would be loth to slay them ere they waked.
How beautiful they seemed !
I think it was their beauty stayed my hand,
More than their slumber.
Yet is sleep sacred too no less than beauty :
But oh, most sacred when its spell holds bound
Loveliness pure as that I gazed on here.
Had these been men, I could not slay them so.
But foolish weakness here were such remorse.
The beauty of angels is the pride of God,
Whereby man's pride He mocks and puts to shame :
Therefore I will not spare it but destroy.
I will go in and slay them where they lie.

> [*He goes back to the tent, and enters. A
> moment later a groan is heard faintly.
> Soon* FRIMUTEL *reappears bearing a sword
> red with blood.*

I have done it. They are dead—both dead.

Who would have thought it ? Yet 'tis so :
Like common men they bleed, they gasp for
    breath,
Then lie quite still.
Only they seem in death more calm, more fair.
Would I had strangled them ! It was ill done
So to wound, so to stain such limbs, such breasts !
But one stirred murmuring in his sleep, and I
Snatched up this sword and smote him to the
    heart.
He scarcely moaned, yet straight the other waked,
And, as I raised my sword, in his scared eyes—
Strange !—I beheld something, I knew not what,
As though remembered from a great while
    since.
Methought I long ago had known those eyes,
Nay, been their lover once—kissed them to sleep.

> *[He stands awhile in meditation. Suddenly a
> loud thunder-clap bursts overhead.*

Ho ! Storms Thine anger now ?
At length dost Thou draw near ?
Lag not upon Thy way.
Behold this crimson witness of my deed !
Haste hither to avenge Thy servants' blood.

> *[Figures are seen hurrying to and fro between
> the tents in the background.*

A Voice

Oh treason, treason! The King's sons are slain!

Frimutel

Ho! Dost Thou hear them, O Thou King of
   kings?
Thou Father of Heaven's host! Slain are Thy
   children!

A Voice

Horror, oh horror! Haste we to rouse the King!

Frimutel

Aye, rouse Him, rouse Him, slaves! I fear Him
   not.
I am His foe. How long must I await Him!
   [*A vivid flash, accompanied by a terrible clap
      of thunder.*
Out of the North break like a sword, bright terror!
Out of the storm-cloud's womb,
O Majesty, O Power,
Be Thou revealed! I fear Thee not, not I.
I am your foe Frimutel.
   [*The* King *enters hurriedly from the back-
      ground, surrounded by Knights and Soldiers.*

27.

VOICES

VOICES

The King!   The King!

FRIMUTEL

Now,   now   He   comes!—Ha!   Can   this   be
    He?

KING

What dreadful outcry scares us from our rest
More hideous than the storm?   What means this
    tumult?
Speak, thou our great deliverer :
Doth then some remnant of our vanquished foe,
Rallied for desperate onslaught, range our tents
And slay us while we sleep?   Speak, I adjure
    thee.
Why dost thou stare upon me with wild eyes
Amazed, distraught?   What means that bloody
    sword
Held naked in thy hand?   Oh speak, speak !

FRIMUTEL (*bursting into loud mad laughter*)

Ha, ha, ha !
Oh fie, false Heavens!   Whom here have ye sent
    me ?

Thou labouring storm-cloud, what, is this your
  birth?
This lark, this prating magpie, this fine jay!

KING

What man art thou that dar'st to mock me
  thus?

FRIMUTEL

What man am I? I am no man, thou knave.
Yet thus much will I tell thee: from the
  race
Of godlike Lucifer, thence am I sprung:
Mine was his pride, his crime and his defiance;
Mine too shall be his glory and his doom.

BYSTANDERS

Blasphemy! Blasphemy!
He hath a devil.   Let him be slain, O King!

FRIMUTEL (*musingly*)

A King?   Was I not once a King?
There was a time—
I have dreamt many things—
Surely it was but dreaming: since how else?—

Among earth's kings none mightier—
Frimutel was he called : the Grail was his.
Why did he sell it to the Devil in Hell?
Aye, sold it for a woman's love, poor fool!
For now they say he hath lost her—
Ah Frimutel, poor wretch !—
Lost his love, and lost his own soul too—
Ah noble Frimutel !

KING

If thou art Frimutel,
Then art thou lost indeed.

A KNIGHT

My lord, an evil spirit is in this man.
Come, let us slay him, lest he work more woe.

KING

Forbear !   Was not this man Heaven's chosen
    servant ?
In God's hand, not in ours, let his fate lie.
        [*Thunder in the distance.   The storm is now
            passing away.*

FRIMUTEL

Oh, ho! Where art thou now?
Canst thou not bide, thou nimble grass-hopper?
Where art thou hiding? Whither hast thou
    flown?
Whence does thy laughter mock me from afar?
Let me come at thee, coward!

> [*A flash of lightning in the distance.*
>
> > Ah, there! there!

Yonder through the clouds thy bright sword plays!
Now bide thou still. I will be with thee soon.

> [*He rushes out madly in the direction of the
> lightning.*

BYSTANDERS

Let him not go! Close on him: smite him down!

KING

Let no man stir! This is the hand of God.

A KNIGHT

My lord, thy woe thou know'st not yet: thy sons—

KING

Ah me! What wouldst thou tell me?

KNIGHT

                                    The young men
Thy sons are slain.

KING

Slain ! Ah speak ! Not slain !

KNIGHT

Alas! I know no other word.   His hands
That slew them thou hast seen, red with their
    blood.

KING

Both ! Yet say not both !

KNIGHT

We will pursue him, and avenge their death.

KING

Nay, let him go.   This is from God, to whom
It hath seemed good to afflict both him and me.
How profitless and vain were vengeance here !
Come, lead me where they lie.

THE END OF THE FIRST ACT

ACT II

A large room in the palace. On a couch to the right
   HERZELOIDA *lies sleeping. One of her waiting-*
   women is sitting at a little distance from her.
   Another of her women comes in from the left,
   and approaches the couch.

FIRST LADY

Softly, softly tread ! See, she is sleeping !
Nay, do not go too near : thy step may wake her,
Thy shadow or the rustling of thy dress.
Come sit here by me : let us speak quite low.

SECOND LADY

Poor fevered soul, may happy sleep awhile
Cheat thee of thy despair : kind be thy dreams :
Nay, like some magic dream-change, may thy fate
Soon turn to smiles its now so frowning brow.

FIRST LADY

Alas ! can any glad change happen here ?
Heart-wounds so deep as these how can Time
    heal ?
Or to the stricken conscience how give peace ?
Save some new fatal birth of woe from woe
What now can Time bring forth ?   Alas ! alas !
That here for evil only Time is strong !

SECOND LADY

Nay, sister, hope beseems us rather here.
Her child is cared for well, in trusted hands,
Far from the town, 'mid simple peasant folk :
Its foster-mother is discreet and honest :
The woman she sends hither from the farm
With word of how from day to day it fares,
Is wise and secret : and save these none else
Have knowledge of the truth, nor ever need.

FIRST LADY

Since last the woman came, thrice hath the night
Crept sleepless on to day, three days have mocked
Forlorn hope's longing eyes, yet still no word
To calm the sick disquiet of her fear.

May it not be the woman with good cause
Thinks it not wise to be seen to and fro
Coming and going every day alike
About what honest business no man knows?

FIRST LADY

'Tis like enough she will use wariness,
Lest curious eyes suspect : and well they may :
There is a pride, a strangeness in her bearing
That sorts not well with homely peasant birth.
She speaks her thought to no man : her replies
Are brief and subtle, baffling forward tongues.
Heaven grant she be not taken for a witch.
Ill would she fare once evil whispers reached
The priest Thaddæus' ears : the princess even,
Plead she to save her ne'er so well and wisely,
Might scarcely then avail.

SECOND LADY

                Heaven grant no harm
Befall her, most for our dear lady's sake,
Whose trust and love, I know not by what art,
She so hath won that some content, some peace
Come ever with her coming, and too oft
With her go hence.

FIRST LADY

Ah, would she were now returned !
For meantime wild and wilder grows her grief.
Not for her child alone she pines, but oft,
Through lips scarce seen to stir, I hear her
  murmur
That dread name we know well yet dare not speak.
And much I fear lest in her sleep, which oft
Will wildly gossip things best left unsaid,
Or waking in some desperate fit, she prove
Unsecret of her trouble before ears
Less charitable than ours, or less discreet.

HERZELOIDA (*murmuring in her sleep*)

Frimutel !   No Frimutel !   Not so !
Stay ! spare them !   See how young they are !

FIRST LADY

Hark !   What saith she ?   'Tis some evil dream.
Were it not best to wake her ?

SECOND LADY

No, let her be.
I know a way to scatter these fierce dreams,
Yet wake her not ; for I will sing a charm

To woo and flatter gentle sleep to stay,
Drowsy as sleep itself.

(*She sings*)

Go not away, Sleep !
Oh, go not yet !
When thou are gone, Sorrow will wake and keep
These eyelids wet.
And is not Sorrow thine enemy, O kind Slumber?
Have ye not striven together times without
    number ?
Will he not ever be plotting against thee ? Nay,
When thou hast vanquished Sorrow, then, even
    then
He bideth his time and will enter stealthily
    creeping
Into the dreaming hearts of men ;
And when they wake their eyes are weeping.

Stay yet awhile, stay !
Awhile keep grief afar.
Thou shalt not say me nay.
I know a charm to beguile thee, for I will say
What sweet things likest are
To thee, sweet Sleep :—the hum of bees in the
    clover;
Indolent waves breaking over and over,

37

Each ere it breaketh pausing long as it can :
And when upon the care-vexed heart of man
Thou fallest, soft is thy coming as snow-flakes fall
On rough bleak moors, settling silently, slowly,
Mantling in smoothness all :
Such is thy coming, Sleep, so still, so holy.

First Lady

Thou hast waked her, see ! Thy fine charms to
    bind sleep
Have only charmed and frighted sleep away.

Herzeloida (*waking*)

Is she not come ? How cruel grow my fears !
What can have chanced ? Ah me ! Another day
Steals towards its evening and she comes not yet.

Second Lady

Nay, fear not ; she will come : 'tis now but noon.
Believe me, scarce one hour have you been
    sleeping.

Herzeloida

Why then my sleep, by many, many hours,
Has been more brief than for its dreams it ought.
Oh, I have had such dreams, had they been waking

Such ages long, so fearful did they seem,
Well might they strew white hairs upon my head.
Yet in my latest visions hope with despair
Was blent so strangely, that I scarce may know
What it should bode.

SECOND LADY

   Such doubts, when shared with friends,
Oft in the very telling grow more clear.

HERZELOIDA

Well thus it was. Methought I found myself
Amid green scented lawns, girt round about
With mighty trees, a spacious forest glade,
Which eve with calm and golden beauty filled,
Even as my heart was filled with tranquil joy
To watch my baby playing at my feet,
Eagerly stretching little fingers out
To clutch the wild flowers by their stalks and pull
Their gay heads close for kisses, bites and smiles.
Around us herds of deer browsed unafraid,
Or on the glade's edge strained their long necks
  high
To reach the lowest leaves with curling tongue.
All cares had wholly gone from me, all sadness ;

39

My babe, the flowers, the sunshine and the beauty
Of those wild creatures wholly could employ
My heart with pleasure, till it seemed as though
I too in that free woodland life had share,
Grown native to their dappled commonwealth.
Suddenly this strange thing befell : there came
A faint sound as of horns ; and all the herd
With ears erect and wide-spread nostrils stood
Astrain for instant flight : me too no less
Like panic seized : and now, man, horse and
    hound,
We saw them sweeping towards us through the
    trees,
And straightway with a dreamer's certainty
I knew that in the midst my father rode
Urging the chase, ranging in wrath to find
And slay his sinful child.   Oh then, my heart
Thrilled through with terror, mindless of my babe,
Mingling among the flying herd (Ah strange !
Even in a dream most strange !) I fled transformed,
No more a woman but a hind, and all
My beauty, that had cost me so much shame,
Degraded to the likeness of a beast.
Scarce yet for terror conscious of my change
Awhile I fled, marvelling at my own fleetness.
But when the hunt no more was heard, and night

Darkened the wood-ways, then first I bethought
      me
Of my lost babe, and wandering to and fro
Long time I sought, in vain, till sick of heart,
In utter weariness, I laid me down.
When daylight came, lo, 'twas the self-same glade
Whence I had fled, and there still lay my babe
Near me asleep.   Oh then what happiness
Was mine !   But, alas ! soon from my changed
      lips,
That strove to lisp " Dear son ! Sweet son ! " the
      words
In senseless moans died off ! Aghast, heart-stricken,
I dared not break his sleep.   Yet soon his eyes
Opening smiled up without fear upon me,
As though he knew his wretched mother still.
So there, how long I know not—yet it seemed
Days grew to weeks, while in that glade alone
We two together dwelt ; and there he fed
Willingly at my breast, so that I soon
Forgot in loving cares my grief and shame.

SECOND LADY

Take comfort ; for such dreams are surely good
That after weeping yet in gladness end.

HERZELOIDA

Alas, not so it ended; for one day
Browsing within the forest I espied
From tree to tree stealthily gliding towards me,
A shaft already notched on the taut string,
Him for whose sake this penance I endured;
Aye, it was he indeed!
Then spite my heart's wild terror, love and hope
Counselled to feign I saw not, and, as though
I sought new pasture, gently lead him on
With easy paces towards the child, that haply,
Beholding him with his wild foster-mother,
He so might take some pity on us both.
But what thereafter might have chanced, I know not,
For there my dream fled, and I trembling waked.

FIRST LADY

See! the woman comes! She is more wise
And skilful in such matters than are we.
Tell her thy dream, and bid her read its meaning.

HERZELOIDA

Now Heaven give me strength to hear her tidings!
    [*To* KUNDRY, *who has entered from the left.*
How late thou comest! Say, is all well?

42

KUNDRY

Aye, well
As Heaven would have it. I pray thee now awhile
Bid that thy women leave us here alone,
For I would speak with none but thee.

  [*The* PRINCESS *signs to her women, who with-
   draw.*

HERZELOIDA

Ah, Kundry,
Now I perceive thou hast ill news to tell.
What has befallen ? How is it with the child ?

KUNDRY

Fret not thy heart so ; for the child is well ;
Nay, there is hope that thou wilt see it soon.

HERZELOIDA

Oh, tell me how ! Couldst thou bring that to pass,
Ah then indeed what joy were mine !

KUNDRY

Yet first
Great peril and much toil must thou endure.
Now listen calmly. Far hence many a mile,
On a wild glen-side, whither no path leads

43

The shepherd's feet, there is a cave deep-set
'Neath brows of jutting rock o'ergrown with ivy,
Sheltered by crowding trees on either hand,
While to the front the wood breaks back a space,
And leaves a green and level glade, made bright
With flowers of every kind that love the sun ;
And from a clear well by the cavern's mouth
A little swift brook hurries through the grass.
Yet thither, to their wonted haunt of old,
But seldom from the thicket and by stealth
Do the shy deer now venture forth to drink
And browse their fill, since in that place dwells one
In form a man, yet whom, had they but sense
And feeling for such woe, even the beasts
Might pity, thus by God and man abandoned,
Outcast, degraded, with changed heart, and thoughts
Uncertain, dim and abject as their own.

HERZELOIDA

Ah, Kundry, hast thou found him ? Hast thou
    seen
Him whom my sin hath made beyond all men
Lost and most woeful ? Know'st thou where he
    dwells,
Oh, take me to him, lead me quickly thither,

44

That I, who shared his guilt, no more henceforth
May in his penance be divided from him.
It may be my remorse hath found some grace,
Some pity in Heaven's sight, and that my love
(Since for one thus afflicted and brought low
Love surely now were charity, not sin)
By tender care and patience may do much
To alleviate the dark misery of his lot.
Nay, how know we but so by Heaven's mercy
I be not destined now to bring back light
To his blind soul, and to his heart repentance?

KUNDRY

It is most noble in thee to scorn fear,
And willingly at hazard of thy life
Thus to adventure for his sake alone.
But when thou hast heard that which must yet be
    told,
Dull wouldst thou be of heart and faint thy courage,
Didst thou but pause or shrink back then.   But thee
How should I doubt!

HERZELOIDA

        Nay, doubt me not, but tell
What yet remains; then set we quickly forth.

Long time, unseen myself, from the wood's edge
I watched him sitting near the cavern's mouth
Motionless as a withered tree long dead,
Whose stiff boughs stir no more to any wind.
So tranced he sat : yet through his eyes' gaunt
    stare
His wildered soul strained forth as though far off
Beyond the clouds it ever sought in vain
What it might nowhere find : and thence I knew
His madness was not parted from him yet.
At length it seemed his ear had caught some sound
I heard not from my hiding mid the trees,
For starting on a sudden he looked down,
His troubled brows grew clearer and he smiled,
Then rose and passed from sight within the cave.
But I, much wondering now what it might be,
(For nothing saw I else save some few goats
That without fear browsed in the rock's cool
    shade
As though domestic there) while he was gone,
Stole quickly nearer, till in the deep grass
Couched soft and warm what think you that I
    saw ?—
A child, a little infant child, that wept

As if just waked.   Then was I glad, for now
I knew what all day long I sought was found,
Thine own lost child.

HERZELOIDA

What, Kundry !   My lost child !
How lost ?   But ah, say first, where is it now ?
Didst thou not save it ?

KUNDRY

Such was my first thought,
To take the child and flee, when suddenly
He came forth from the cave ; so I lay still
To watch what he might do.   But when I saw
How tenderly, with what a patient care,
He calmed its grief and stilled its hungry cries
With goatsmilk from his cave, then my worst fears
Grew quiet : yet I dared not venture nigh,
Lest seeing me his madness might break forth,
And he should slay me ere I told my tale.
So there I left him and sped back to thee.
But in those pathless wilds, when dusk came on,
I lost my way and wandered half the night,
Else with the break of day had I been here.

HERZELOIDA

But how came he to know the child was his?

KUNDRY

Alas, too well, as I have told thee oft,
From my own lips he knew that bitter doom
Reserved for him and his, whereof some shadow,
Through his bewildered soul obscurely working,
Hath made him seek until he found the child.
Twice have we gone together to the farm:
It may be from some hiding near our path
He watched us pass, then followed us afar,
Surmising on what purpose we were bound.
So it must be; for once indeed I saw him,
Where the track leaves the thicket for the fields:
From beneath matted locks with gaunt fierce gaze
He glared upon me, then, as in wrath or scorn,
Stalked from me through the trees.   Hence, when
    I heard
How some about the farm that day had seen
A strange wild madman clad in skins of beasts,
Yet took but slight heed then, and how soon after
The child was missed, then straightway I resolved
To search the forest far and near, nor cease
Till I had found him.   How I sped, thou hast heard.

HERZELOIDA

Ah Kundry, well and wisely hast thou done.
How may I thank thee for thy noble zeal!
But let us now make ready to set forth.
How my heart sinks at thought of what might
　　chance
Should his mood change while we still linger here!
Ah me, those cruel words that night and day
Knell ever through my soul: "Destroy thy child,
Or he shall destroy thee"—should but once
Their dreadful import like a returning flood
After long ebb surge back upon his mind,
Alas, what horrible fulfilment then
Might Heaven's doom find! O Kundry, let us
　　haste!

KUNDRY

Nay, rather trust God will not suffer now
Thine innocent child to perish, but through him
Designs to bless both Frimutel and thee.

HERZELOIDA ►

Could he repent—might I not hope, then,
That all mercy Heaven would not withhold,
But of his doom one misery remit
Worst and most dire?

KUNDRY

Such be thy hope ; and now
May it bring ease and comfort to' thy grief :
For thou hast need of rest, ere with first dawn
To-morrow we set forth.

HERZELOIDA

Oh why not now—
This very night ?   How far off seems to-morrow !

KUNDRY

We must not go by night ; for then the way
Were hard to find : by day I cannot fail.

> [*A Page followed by two peasants in rough
> shepherd's dress come in from the left.
> Behind them re-enter the two waiting-
> women.   The younger of the shepherds
> bears a basket of plaited reeds.*

PAGE

Step forward, sirs !   This way to the King's
presence !

SHEPHERD

Nay, these be ladies' chambers.   'Tis not meet
For plain folk such as we to trespass here.
Come, mock us not, but do as you were bid,
And lead us straight, I pray you, to the King.

PAGE

Alas, what simple folk these shepherds be !
This is indeed the straight way to the throne.
Kings' houses are not built like shepherds' cots.

SHEPHERD

Nay then, I'll go no further.
Upstairs and down we've followed him this hour,
Round and about through fifty different doors,
Down passages and halls we know not whither.

WAITING-WOMAN

Whom do you seek, shepherds ?

SHEPHERD

                       Madam, the King :
'Tis him we fain would see.

PAGE

       Well, let them show
('Tis all I ask) what lies within their basket :
Then will I lead straight on the nearest way.

SHEPHERD

Nay, that we must not. 'Tis for the King's eyes,
The King's alone.

WAITING-WOMAN

     Come, though you show it not,
Yet look you, shepherds, what harm can be done
By the mere telling ?

SHEPHERD

      I know not that. Our tale
Must first be told in royal ears.

PAGE

       How say you ?
" In royal ears ! " Is not the princess here ?
What want you more ? Come, let her have your
  tale.

WAITING-WOMAN

Tell it, good friends, so it be worth our hearing.

SHEPHERD

Aye, that it is, and marvellous as 'tis true—
A very portent, none e'er saw its like :
And to my thinking it were better burned,
This devil's urchin, ere it can bring mischance ;
For sure there's witchcraft and the fiend's work
    here.
Did ever any son of Adam yet
Behold in the wild forest a man child
Mothered and suckled by a dappled doe ?

WAITING-WOMAN

The Lord have mercy !   What, is that your tale ?

SHEPHERD

Aye, 'tis a strange tale, yet as true as strange.

HERZELOIDA (*coming forward*)

But tell me, shepherds, where did you find the
    child ?
Said you not in the forest ?

SHEPHERD

                          Aye, 'twas there, lady :
The forest of Broceliande men call it ;
Hence many a mile far up among the hills.
There had we gone, my son and I, to seek
Some wandered goats, and there, in a green glade,
Beside a little brook before a cave,
We chanced upon it, naked as a worm
In the warm sun.

HERZELOIDA

                    But saw you none else by ?
Did you not search the cave ? Dwelt no man
    there ?

SHEPHERD

Nay, none that we could see : yet for the cave,
We had no mind to search it ; for how knew we
Within its glooms what foul fiend might inhabit ?
Since at the very mouth—

HERZELOIDA

                       Aye, there it was
You found this child. But say, in what plight
    was it ?—
Weeping and starved ?

SHEPHERD

            Not so ; the witch's brat
Seemed hale enough.   Yet did it fall a-weeping
When its strange mother fled as we came near.

HERZELOIDA

I pray you, shepherd, let me see the child.
Come, let me lift the cloth.

SHEPHERD

              Nay, God forbid !
Thou must not, lady. 'Tis a thing accurst,
Monstrous and evil-eyed, whose very glance
Might draw who knows what mischief on your
    head ? -

HERZELOIDA

Fear not for that. See, I have here a charm,
This silver sprig of branching rue, whose power
Can well preserve my life from all such harms,
And make its glance for me as innocent
As though I were its mother. Come, let me
    look.

SHEPHERD

I like it not. But how to say thee nay !
Well, take thy look.

> [*The younger shepherd sets the basket down
> upon the couch. The* PRINCESS, *kneeling
> beside it, lifts a cloth that covers the child,
> and, after a short silence, speaks.*

HERZELOIDA

Alas, poor outcast wretch !
Frail, luckless blossom of humanity,
Untimely venturing on a world unkind !
How like an unfledged bird, by ruthless hands
Robbed whence it nestled 'neath its mother's
    breast,
Hast thou come here perforce, without thy will,
Whither and whence to thee unknown ! Ah,
    surely
Hadst thou within the darkness of the womb
Foreknown what misery should await thee here,
Then never to behold the light of day
Thou wouldst have longed. Nay, better had it
    been
If by thy birth thou then hadst slain thy mother
That bore thee to thy sorrow and her own.

Think it not strange, kind shepherds, that I weep,
As though I were its mother, o'er this child.
A woman's heart is ever prompt to tears :
And tenderness came o'er me now, at thought
How bitter, how forlorn his lot must be,
Should he live on to boyhood without name,
Friendless and motherless.   Alas, poor innocent !
Let me then be thy mother !   Wouldst thou so ?
See, it smiles back as though to give consent !
(Rising)
Then, shepherds, let me take it for my own.
Grudge me not this.   I will reward you well.

SHEPHERD

What thing is this thou hast asked of us !   Nay, lady,
Never could we consent to grant you that.

HERZELOIDA

But why not, shepherd ?   I will give you gold.
From this day forth you shall be poor no more.

SHEPHERD

Nay, lady, keep thy gold.   We be honest men.
We did not well at first to gossip so,
And ill indeed to let thee see its face.

57

Sure thou art overlooked for all thy charms,
Since thou canst crave to rear this imp of evil.
'Tis good time now we brought it to the King.
He has no love for witches nor their brats.

HERZELOIDA

Is there no pity in you?   If there be,
Oh, let it wake now, shepherd.   Nay, thy trade
Is merciful, and should have taught thee pity.
Canst thou be tender to your new born lambs,
Yet harden so your heart against this foundling
Of your own kind?   What harm hath it done to you,
Or can it do to me?   How have you warrant
To condemn it thus as an unnatural birth,
Because you found it in the woods, and saw
How a wild beast more pitiful than you
Had pity on it?   I beseech you, sirs,
Bethink you who I am entreats you thus.

SHEPHERD

Lady, to thee we mean no disrespect;
Nevertheless we can but say thee nay.
'Tis plain the bairn's glance hath bewitched thy
    heart,
That thou canst pity what thou shouldst abhor,

58

And even deniest what is so manifest,
That there is witchcraft here.   Then, lest it work
More mischief, come, let us begone forthwith.
Sentence be with the King : his will be done.

HERZELOIDA

Alas, can superstition
So change man's heart to stone!   Stay, I entreat you!
Inhuman peasants, I command you, stay !
>   [*The shepherds have again taken up the basket,
>   and now go out to the right, preceded by
>   the page.*   KUNDRY *restrains* HERZE-
>   LOIDA, *who makes as though she would
>   follow them.*

KUNDRY

Have patience, I beseech you.   Let them go,
Since go they will.   Seek not to call them back,
Nor waste more words upon them, lest you seem
Beyond all need importunate and eager.
Rather take thought what thou shalt speak and do
When thou art come before thy father's throne
To plead for the child's life.   Oh take heed then
Lest you betray yourself by act or word.
Be resolute and calm ; such eloquence
Will most persuade and be suspected least.

HERZELOIDA

Ah, doubt not but that love shall school my tongue,
And prompt it to all subtlety and cunning.
Yet how bitter to have seemed so near,
To have seen and hoped, then to have lost once
    more !
And now with guilt and fear at heart to plead
Before my father thus for my own child
As for some casual boon, forced to stoop low
To sophistries and lies, to speak all things
Save the truth only !

KUNDRY

Nay, 'tis no time for scruples.   But come now,
That first I may array thee as befits,
And meantime give thee counsel, lest it chance
Thy suit should fail.

HERZELOIDA

    Alas, what then remains
Save to make known my shame ?

KUNDRY

     Art thou prepared
To die ?

HERZELOIDA

   How gladly would I welcome death
If so my child might live !
But no, it cannot be my suit should fail.

KUNDRY

I think thou canst not fail,
Yet may no priest stand near the throne to-day
Like a dark shadow to scare mercy thence.

HERZELOIDA

Thaddæus dost thou mean ? Thy fears are true.
Alas, how many infamies of late
In witchcraft's hateful name have stained our land
Through this man's counsels ! O just God,
Why to mere names, forged void of truth, by man's
Own wickedness and folly, hast thou given
Such power to make foul havoc of this earth
Created to thy glory once so fair,
And peopled with a race after thine image ?
Oh pardon me my sin : look down with pity
On this thine innocent child ; and for his sake
Guide thou my tongue, and strengthen my weak
  heart
With wisdom's might in this dread trial's hour.

THE END OF THE SECOND ACT

ACT III

A hall in the palace. The KING *is seated upon his throne, surrounded by counsellors and officials of his court. At his right hand stands the priest* THADDÆUS, *and before him the two* SHEPHERDS. *The basket with the infant is laid on the ground at their feet.*

KING

But thou, Thaddæus, what say'st thou of this?

THADDÆUS

O King, here is no need for doubt at all.
Out of the mouths of these poor simple shepherds
The truth hath been declared, since, as they say,
This strange unnatural birth is a dark sign
Portentous of some dire calamity
Threatening this realm, and doubtless soon to fall
Had not Heaven's grace by this most happy chance
Forewarned us to avert the coming doom

By sacrifice to the consuming flames
Of this ill-omened progeny of hell,
As of a thing accurst.   Then may you hope,
Through mediation of His holy priesthood,
Still to prevent the imminent wrath of God.

KING

Is there no other way, more merciful,
More just than this?   If verily God's wrath
Threatens the state, then must we seek the cause,
Which surely will be found some general sin,
By public prayer and penance best atoned.
Or if it be some hidden crime, whereof
Greatness is guilty, then, though near our throne,
Aye, next my very heart, they shall not 'scape
The stroke of justice.   But, whate'er the offence,
Wherein should this poor babe, being but the mute
And guiltless instrument of Heaven's warning,
Merit a fate so cruel at our hands?
>   [*The* PRINCESS HERZELOIDA *enters, followed by*
>   *her two waiting-women and* KUNDRY.

THADDÆUS

O King, beware lest thy too generous heart
Should be beguiled by fair appearing shows
Of specious clemency, thus fatally

To oppose your will against the general welfare,
And God's clear purpose here by me declared.
Because His providence led on these men
To find this infant, dost thou deem for that
It is His angel, sent by Him from heaven,
Brought forth and suckled by a beast of the
    field ?
Nay that were then no prodigy at all;
Yet none can doubt that such it is. Doth God
Delight in miracles so vain, or stoop
His power to counterfeit the devil himself?
Either this is from Heaven or from Hell;
And if it be from Hell (as who can question ?)
Why then there is no place for pity here.
Thus I advise, let it be burned forthwith,
So shall thyself and the whole state be saved.

KING

So be it then according to thy counsel.
In such dark lore thou art more wise than we.

HERZELOIDA (*coming forward*)

Pardon me, father, if at an hour untimely
I break upon your counsels : but I come
To crave a boon too urgent for delay.

KING

Name thy request, dear child.   All within reason
That thou canst ask is granted thee already.

HERZELOIDA

Then thou wilt grant it; since my theme is
    mercy :
And is not mercy reason's eldest child?
Hath this poor hapless spark of life, which God's
Own loving hand has lit—hath it had none
To plead one word why it should not be quenched
Utterly without hope to be rekindled?
Then will I plead for thee, since thou canst not,
Nor canst so much as one word understand
Of that too stern, too hasty sentence passed
But now upon thine innocent head.   Father,
Call back what thou hast said.   Yes, I beseech
    you,
Spare the child's life.   Ah, wherefore need it die?

KING

Child, thy petition would become thee well
To ask, and me to grant—were it but possible.
But then what need could rise for thee to sue?

Could I condemn to the flames a harmless babe
Wantonly, without cause? Nay, God forbid!
We are not so inhuman. But Thaddæus,
As you have heard but now, has given us reasons
Serious and wise for this.

HERZELOIDA

    Alas, what reasons?
Methinks he said to save the state from ruin.
What ruin? Can a tender new-born babe
Lay waste a kingdom? or this little hand,
That scarce can crush a gnat, take human life,
Or make one mother childless save its own?
For the wild hind of which these shepherds
  spake,
(For all they saw or thought they saw) nor is
Nor ever could be mother to this child.
How it came there I know not, but I know
Neither is this from Hell, nor yet from Heaven,
But from the womb of sinful woman born,
Even as I and all the world alike,
To sorrow sorrowfully brought forth. Then
  why
Add needless unto necessary woe?
Wherefore withhold your pity in a world
So poor in pity, yet with so great need?

THADDÆUS

Alas, how blind, how liable to error
Is woman's pitying heart that reason guides not !
Lady, I praise thy charitable intent,
Yet cannot praise thy wisdom. How shouldst
    thou,
By what authority, make bold to set
Thy judgment against ours, declaring this
To be no prodigy ? Whence came thy know-
    ledge ?
Such knowledge only to His holy priesthood
By God is given ; and shalt thou presume
To question what through their lips He com-
    mands ?

HERZELOIDA

And doth our loving Father, who hath said
I will have mercy, and not sacrifice—
Aye, and hath said that whoso shall offend
One of His little ones, 'twere best a mill-stone
Were hanged about his neck, and he were cast
In the sea's depths—doth God indeed command
This infamous thing ? Are you that bid do this
His priesthood ? Oh then may He change, I pray,
And soften your hard hearts, and make that light
Which now is dark indeed !

KING (*angrily*)

Herzeloida !

HERZELOIDA

Alas, what have I said !
Nay then, forgive me, father.
'Twas pity, grown too passionate, awhile
Made me forget that due respect I owe.
Henceforth calmly and humbly will I plead.
Consider then, ere thus, on the bare word
Of these rude peasants you condemn this child.
How know you they speak truth, or for gain's sake
Have forged this tale ?   Yet grant their witness
      true
What then ?   Why nought but this :
That when they found the child a deer fled thence.
In the wild woods is that a portent ?—Nay,
But 'twas a doe, they say, and gave it suck.
Even wise and honest eyes err oftentimes ;
And when doth superstition see truth clear ?
But grant that too for truth : what follows thence ?
Even the beasts of the field show charity
Where man has none.   There is example for it.
Did not the she-wolf suckle Rome's first kings ?
Was that an evil portent ?   Nay, those paps
Surely were blest of Heaven : by that fierce milk

The whole world was ennobled and made strong.
May it not then here too have likewise chanced
That some unhappy woman, shame constraining,
Exposed the child she had no heart to kill,
So to conceal her guilt ?   Surely such things
Have often been before.   Then why not now ?
Is it not best, conforms it not more wisely
To our weak human reason, that then most
Should please God when it least presumes to
    measure
What lies beyond its knowledge—is it not better
In humbleness of heart so to conceive,
Than thus in superstition's name (for surely
This cannot be religion) to do that
Which else had seemed a crime beyond all others
Foul and abhorred ?

THADDÆUS

       Think you I can stand by
And suffer such things to be said ?   Know then,
(And having heard dispute no more in vain)
Know that for trial of man's sinful nature,
By just and all-wise sufferance of God,
Unto the powers of Hell there hath been given
Divided empire with Him through the world.
Therefore at sundry times, in sundry places,

Even as God to bless mankind hath oft
Changed Nature's wonted ordinance to perform
His signs and miracles, so likewise Satan
Delighteth to work wonders manifold,
Sorceries to afflict and plague man's body,
Witchcrafts to tempt his soul, dark prodigies,
Such as you here behold, threatening whole realms
With ruin if not forthwith purged by fire,
And the malignant spirit, tenanting
This fair disguise of human flesh, dislodged,
And houseless sent, whence it came forth, to Hell.
By science sure and certain this we know
Who are His priests.   This to deny and doubt
Is heresy indeed.

HERZELOIDA

For such a heresy
How willingly could I lay down my life !
Look on this babe, behold its tender beauty
Sordidly cradled, swaddled in coarse rags,
Yet for all that so fair ! Ah, surely, father,
In loveliness so sweet and pure as this
Resides a power, a dignity that mocks
And puts to shame all proud and cruel thoughts.
Nay, beauty is the smile upon God's face,
And, like sun glances piercing the rent clouds,

Everywhere and forever breaketh forth
Through the world's veil that hides Him from
    man's eyes
Too weak to endure His perfect glory yet.
Thus doth God's love reveal itself to man.
Nevertheless proud man regardeth not,
But blinded by presumptuous superstition
Curseth and would destroy what God has made,
As though He made it not.   Hath not His will
Created all things both in heaven and earth,
And to the sun and stars assigned their courses,
Its bounds and motions to the sea ?   His law
Appointeth in what season each green thing
Shall for man's service put forth fruit and flower,
Aye, and ordains what time sweet love shall fall
On heart of beast or bird or man, that each
Conceiving may bring forth after his kind.
Nor yet thereafter doth God's providence
Forsake His children, but His power forthwith
Èntering anew within the mother's heart
Sets new love there to cherish and sustain
Tenderly at her breast the life she gave.
If therefore God's almighty law alone
Governs all nature, if without His will
Nought can be born into the light of day,
Nought grow to strength and loveliness—shall man,

Of all His creatures loved and favoured most,
Conceive within his soul a thought so vain
As to deny God's infinite power and doubt
His love and goodness? Since what do ye else
Maintaining this to be no child of God,
But Satan's evil offspring? Either then
Doth Satan's malice triumph o'er God's power,
Or God himself hath failed in goodness here,
Suffering this evil which His power might thwart.
Are not such doubts folly and worse than folly?
For over man's corruptible soul indeed
Satan may have dominion : but that thus
He can defeat God's loving will—alas !
What doctrine vain and blasphemous were that !

Still dost thou frown? Ah, father, if my tongue
Grown overbold hath given offence once more,
Believe 'twas not presumption, no, not that—
But so I speak as heart and reason prompt,
Too earnestly perchance through lack of art,
But not through wilful pride. See, he has waked !
Poor wretch, he weeps. Even so wept
The babe whom Pharaoh's daughter floating found
In bullrush ark, and pitying saved, as I
Would fain now do. Let me keep silence then.
More feelingly than I these tears should plead.

THADDÆUS

Wilt thou permit before thy very throne
Thy counsellors and priests to be defied,
Browbeaten thus by a presumptuous girl,
Whose overweening tongue would school God's
    priests
In things divine, as though herself, not they,
Alone had knowledge and interpretation
Of God's high mysteries? 'Tis not to be borne.

HERZELOIDA

Are these His holy mysteries? Doth He verily
Like heathen Moloch foully take delight
In blood of human babes and mothers' tears?

KING

Insolent child, check thy reviling tongue:
Keep silence; for no more will we endure
Thy stubborn pride, lest thou shouldst soon provoke
Worse than our mere displeasure and rebuke.
Is this that docile maidenly discretion
It was our pride to praise? Have flattering tongues
Of silly waiting-women wrought this change?
Or whence this strange perverseness to oppose
Thine ignorance to wisdom's grave authority?

73

Now quit my presence, child.
Shepherds, lift up your burden,
And bear it where Thaddæus shall give order.

[*The* PRINCESS *throws herself at the* KING's *feet.*

Cling not about my garments. Rise, I command
  you.

HERZELOIDA

Not till thou grant my prayer.
Oh hear me, father, yet.
Turn not thy face away.
Some respite yet, some little respite only !
'Tis all I ask—to help truth shine forth clear.
That wretched unknown mother could not plead
With a more heart-felt passion than I do
To save her child from death, to save thee, father,
From this great shame, our house from infamy
Thou know'st not, canst not guess, but which,
  alas !
I can perceive so clear.

KING

No more !—Get hence !
Out of my sight, I say !—Thou wilt not rise ?

[*Turning to* KUNDRY.

Thou, woman, take her hence.

HERZELOIDA (*rising*)

There is no need, father. Of mine own will,
Thou seest, I will rise, since all proves vain.
Yet one word more I fain would speak ; not such
As need provoke new wrath : grudge not to hear
    me.
Father, I would confess, 'twas not alone
Mere pity's impulse (yet that too) constrained me
So to plead for this doomed and friendless life :
But now before your throne must I bring one
Who shall confess her guilt and own this child,
The wretched outcast of her sin and sorrow.
For her I braved your anger, for her sake
Endured reproach how bitter ! striving still
To save her child, yet keep concealed her shame :
For even as my very self I loved her.
She will not plead nor strive as I have done.
When like a withered flower she bows before you,
Then punish her transgression as seems just.
Yet not too harshly shalt thou deal with her,
Although so great her sin : for she is one
Whose broken, penitent spirit seeks no more
To extenuate her shame—one who, as in a dream,
A trustful dream's brief vain felicity,
That fears no waking, knows not, takes no thought

Of sin at all, for Love's sake cast away
That without which all else on earth she prized,
Even Love itself, as waking soon she found,
Proves of base worth indeed. Alone her child
Is left her now to love and live for still,
Or, if need be, to die for, and cast off
Her sinful life more readily than I
Cast off this robe, and stand before you thus,
Mourning my shame in raiment black as death,
Death, for whose sentence thus I came prepared.

> [*She has thrown off her outer robes, and
> appears in a black garment.
> A silence follows. At length the* KING *speaks.*

KING

What mean you by these insolent mummeries?
Art thou beside thyself to be refused
Thy scandalous whim? Didst thou come here
    prepared,
When all else failed, to play this shameless part?
Thou fool, what if I took thee at thy word,
And sent thee to an infamous death, thy due
If verily thus our house had been dishonoured!
Soon then wouldst thou deny this devil's bastard,
With craven tears recanting the disgrace
Of thy pretended whoredom, thou vain fool.

Waiting-Woman

My lord, I pray thee, hear thy servant speak.
So far thou mayst believe what she hath said,
That this poor outcast is indeed the child
Of some unhappy woman whom she loved.
Oh then forbear to question further, sire.
Let it rest so.   Thou wouldst not break her
     heart !
Nay, thou hast heard her say that she so loved
This woman, that for her sake she withstood
Your anger, used craft, doubtless must be blamed.
But 'twas her generous heart, that had no thought
Except to shield her friend.   Grown desperate
     now
She speaks and does in truth she knows not what.

Herzeloida

What I have said and done I know full well.
Listen not to this foolish woman, father.
Yet kind and good is her intent, I know.
None but myself am mother to this child.
Think you that I would take this shame upon
     me,
Than death more bitter, falsely, for the sake
Of a child born from any sin save mine ?

KING

If this indeed be truth, speak truth once more.
Thy guiltiness thou hast confessed ; now therefore,
So thou hast hope of mercy for thyself
And for this bastard here, make known his name
Who hath been thy secret paramour, and brought
Thee and all thine to this dishonour.   Speak !

HERZELOIDA

Nay, father, put me not to that last shame:
Spare me this deadliest misery of all.
Seek not to know : for thine own sake forbear.
If I must die, oh let silence be
The grave both of myself and my dishonour !
I plead not now for mercy.   Yea, my life,
Like a stained robe, freely without a murmur
Would I lay off, so I might die assured
That thou wouldst spare my child.
O father, let him live !

KING

Till thou acknowledge whence 'tis born, seek not
To stir compassion for this child.   Not so
For all thy cunning art shalt thou evade
My just demand.   Think'st thou I will consent

To rear this bastard publicly confessed,
Yet not know what vile slave makes it his jest
How he has given a grandchild to his king,
And among base-born fellows boasts thy shame?

HERZELOIDA

That shall they never.   No ignoble slave
Was my child's sire.   Heroes and kings alone
Were fellows to his greatness, ere yet sin
Through me entered his heart, ere yet God's hand
Had touched and brought low Frimutel.

KING (rising)

Oh, horrible!
Dost thou mean him, Frimutel,
The murderer of my sons,
The bane and desolation of our house,
Impious, accurst, apostate,
Abhorred of God and man?   Was it thou then
That didst seduce him to his fall?   Wert thou
Cause both of his sin and our affliction!
Ah, better had the hand that slew thy brothers
That day in his mad frenzy slain thee too;
So hadst thou perished with thy guilt unknown.
Now therefore be thy shame thy punishment.
Well dost thou merit death;

79

Yet thee I cannot slay,
But from my sight forever banish thee.
For this thy child,
Impious rebellion's seed, foul murder's offspring,
Think not that I will suffer it to live.
Thaddæus, take it hence.

Thaddæus

     My lord, beware.
Not so here would I counsel; since perchance
With man it lies not wholly to dispose
Whether this child be now to live or die.
Though through rebellion and in sin conceived,
Yet holy is the race of Titurel.
Over its own invisibly the Grail
Keeps ever watch and ward. What lies beneath
  its care
Let no man seek profanely to destroy.
Thus then I counsel: let command be given
That with its mother now the child be borne
Even to the very spot deep in the vast
And trackless mountain-forest, where these shep-
  herds
Found it exposed—(*Looking towards the* Princess)—
  by whom and to what end
Let us not search too strictly, since from death

'Twas there by strangest miracle preserved.
Abandoned there beyond all human aid
Thus may we leave them to the Grail's own mercy,
According to its secret purposes
So to dispose, whether for life or death,
Both of the child and of its sinful mother.

KING

Thaddæus, wise and timely is thy counsel.
Thus will we do, and so may no reproach,
Neither from Heaven, nor yet in man's report,
Censure us here as tyrannous or unjust.
Herzeloida,
Against thy sentence hast thou aught to say?

HERZELOIDA

No, father, nothing.   If it so seems just
In thy sight, henceforth will I be resigned
To whatsoever for my child and me
Our destiny may bring.   Yet this one boon,
This only, I beseech you, grant me now :
Suffer, if she forsake me not, this woman
                        [*Turning to* KUNDRY.
To come with me, that so in my distress
I yet may be not utterly forlorn,

Nor of all human comfort quite bereft.
Nay, though I there should die, yet may the Grail
Design through her to save my son from death.
Is he not heir to Titurel's holy throne?
Oh then, despite his father's sin and mine,
Nobler and happier destinies than ours
May yet perchance be his.   This last request
Do not deny me, father.

KING

     Be it so then.
If she will follow thee, I forbid her not.
But let none else, on pain of death, go with thee,
Save whom thereto Thaddæus shall appoint :
For to his charge do I commit you now.

THE END OF THE THIRD ACT.

ACT IV

SCENE I

A small glade in the forest. The scene is bordered by trees on either side, and trees shut out the view in the background. To the right in front is a large oak. The ground here and there, especially beneath the trees, is overgrown with ferns and brambles.

The two SHEPHERDS *enter from the left, followed by* THADDÆUS *and* HERZELOIDA, *who is clothed in black robes, as at the end of the last Act. One of the shepherds is carrying the child. The evening twilight has already set in.*

THADDÆUS

Light wanes fast. Come now, shepherds, speak
    truly;
How far yet is it onward to the cave?

SHEPHERD

'Tis best we went no farther.

THADDÆUS

Is this the place then ?

SHEPHERD

Nay ; for some time since
The way was lost, indeed we know not how.
Let us turn back : forward we dare not go,
Lest night creep round us in these unknown glens.

THADDÆUS

Here then set down your burden.
[*The* SHEPHERD *lays the child on the grass
beneath the oak-tree.* THADDÆUS *now
addresses* HERZELOIDA, *who, while he is
speaking, remains motionless, as though
unconscious of his presence.*
Herzeloida,
Ere in this place appointed for thy doom
Alone I leave thee, speak, dost thou indeed
Truly repent that sin for which thy life
Is justly forfeit, nay, thy very soul
If thou shalt not repent ?
[*He pauses for a moment.*

Speak! Why art thou silent?
Ready and bold enough wast thou of tongue
Not long since, when to hide thy shame, yet
    save
Thy bastard from the flames, thou didst contend
Against true doctrine vainly; or when there-
    after,
To stir compassion, subtly thou didst profess
Remorse unfeigned, now by thy stubborn silence
Most easy to be seen how feigned it was.
Or is thy proud heart galled that I forbade
Thy woman pander to attend thee hither,
Thy guilt's confederate? Doubtless thou didst
    trust
Her cunning might avail to save thee here.
Yet her own self not all her witchcrafts now
May save from a foul death, when I return.
Farewell! I leave thee now, whether for life,
Or death. Thine only be the guilt, not ours,
Nor yet thy sire's, if so be that the Grail
Deliver not from death thy son and thee.

      [THADDÆUS *and the* SHEPHERDS *go out to the*
         left. HERZELOIDA *remains standing for*
         a few moments, then turns to her child, and
         kneeling down beside it, gazes awhile in
         silence, and at length speaks.

O my child, my child,
Slumberest thou? And I—
Ah, what despair is mine !
Ignorant of our woe, of death that draweth near
    thee,
Of the tears that from thy mother's face
Over thine own drop down, not for my sake,
Not for mine, but, O my love, for thee,
Heedless of all things save thy sweet dreams only,
Thy little infant heart is sleeping. Nay,
Wert thou to wake, even then
What were despair, what death to thee that canst
    not know them—
Not as I now their bitterness must know,
For thy sake, not for mine, O my child, my child ?

Would that I now might be,
As once in dream's fierce anguish,
A hind of the forest swift and free,
Among the green leaves feeding.
Oh then, my babe, thou and I,
Without a want, without care,
Here would we dwell under the cool trees
Easily as in dream alone we two together.

Men, cruel men, soon would my heart forget :
With woman's form and beauty would pass away
Shame, mine own shame even.
All woeful things, all things ill-done,
As though they had never been would be no more.
Only my love, only, my sweet babe,
Thy mother's love for thee,
That alone should neither cease nor suffer change,
But in the forest here
Beside me wouldst thou grow like a young tree
To strength and beauty year after slow year.—
But then, Ah !
As in my dream's terror he came, so
Terribly now might he come,
Stealthily through the trees creeping upon me,
A cruel arrow laid across his bow,
For the heart that loved, that even in death must
    love him,
In madness to pierce it through.
But thee, child, not thee would he slay—Ah, no,
    no !
Had he so willed already had he slain thee.
Nay, but I do thee wrong to dread thee thus,
O Frimutel, my soul's desire, my longing !
Would that here thou mightest find us, for I have
    faith

That thou wouldst be more pitiful than those
Who cruelly to a cruel death
Hither have cast us forth ;
More pitiful than the forest by whose roots
Our mouldering bodies now shall be devoured,
If thou come not soon,
If some deliverance soon from Heaven appear not.

Holy Mary, mother's fears,
Mother's joy thy heart hath known.
Oh hearken now, and on a mother's tears
Be thy pity shown !
All sweet and gracious qualities
Of womanhood were thine :
Gentle was thy heart and wise ;
Gazing on thy child, thine eyes
Filled with love and joy divine.
Smiles and tears o'er thy face
Came and went, tears to smiling
In a moment giving place,
Mighty hope thy fears beguiling.
Joy and care within thy heart
Oft would thus together dwell :
How the same time to smile and sigh
Thy beauteous mouth knew well :
With loving thought and tenderness

Now one moment it grew gay ;
Now the gentle playful words
From thy lips would die away.
O my child, upon thee gazing
Mine eyes too with tears are filling,
Tears of joy in grief's despite :
In my heart great hopes are stirring ;
Sorrow there is changed to gladness,
O my love, my heart's delight.

See, at length from sleep
Thine eyes unclose !
More dark and dark apace
Though now it grows,
Yet o'er thy face
Soft smiles I see creep,
Soft and kind, as though
Thou my grief didst know,
And fain with a smile
Wouldst my grief beguile.
Nay, little child, glad now am I,
For faith is mine in forest wild
Thou art not destined here to die.
Then grief or gladness, come what may,
No more I pine, I fear no ill,
But wait in hope till break of day.

Nights are not long nor forest chill
If hearts are warm and courage strong.
Sleep then; fear no harm:
Near my breast 'tis safe and warm.
There to sleep is best:
Sweetest dreams come so
On thy mother's breast.

Ah, slow, slow!
Night dark as our woe!
Yet soon the night will go.

Scene II

The same scene as before, in the early morning twilight.
    Herzeloida *is sitting beneath the oak-tree, with*
    the child on her lap.

Art thou awake?   Nay,
Turn yet again to sleep:
'Tis not yet day.
Though under the boughs dawn creep,
And one by one in the leaves above
Each into song the birds are breaking,
Yet still shouldst thou be sleeping; for are not they
More old than thee, my little love,

By many a week and day?
Then sleep though birds be waking.

Wilt thou not sleep?   No?
Then have thy will.
Wouldst thou my breast?   So!
There suck thy fill.
How know I but for thee and me
This our last living joy may be!
Thus let me still thy weeping, and so mayst thou
Turn thee again to rest : but me our woe
Wakeful all night hath kept, and now
The long slow daylight through
Wakeful must still be keeping,
Till soon I too
With thee shall lie sleeping.

> [*She rises and lays the child down on the grass,*
> *where it is hidden from sight by a clump*
> *of ferns.*

Softly now awhile mid long grass laid
Thus let me leave thee.   Haply around this glade
Wandering I may find nuts, berries wild,
Or comb of woodland bee, that so, my child,
We die not yet, be it but one short day.
Ah, there again that sound, that all night long
Mine ear hath caught, whene'er the wind among

The leaves grew still—somewhere not far away,
As of a brook from little pool to pool
Falling with quiet noise.
There may I drink and cool
My lips and brow, while thus beneath the fern
Safely thou sleepest till I soon return.

> [*She goes out towards the background. A little later a doe comes in slowly from the right, and strays, browsing the grass, towards the place where the child is lying. Suddenly* FRIMUTEL *appears in the foreground beneath the trees to the left, clothed in skins of beasts, and bearing a bow with an arrow laid on the string. The doe bounds away, seeking to escape, but* FRIMUTEL *lets fly his arrow, and the doe falls dead among the ferns and brambles beneath the trees towards the right of the back-ground.* FRIMUTEL, *hastening forward, perceives the child and approaches. He speaks, standing over it.*

FRIMUTEL

So, so, poor fool! Here then wast thou hiding?
Poor wanton wretch, '

Thus like a silly worm to creep away !
Sorrowing have I sought thee these three days,
To find thee here consorting with wild beasts.
What shouldst thou know to teach them, or they
    thee ?
When I came back and found thee gone, I thought
Mine enemy had done this thing to plague me.
Oh then I cursed him, cursed him.
Yet though I erred to curse him for a thief,
Not therefore will I ask his pardon now.
He hath done worse, far worse,
Aye, many and many a time.
But thou, my wanton, surely 'tis not for thee
To learn of the shrinking woodmouse and shy mole.
Rather shall the fierce wolf and mountain bear
Teach thy young limbs what first they needs must
    learn
Ere thou art worthy of thy fate and mine,
Aye, nobler than our fate, since thus alone
Both Him and His vengeance may we despise.

Art thou weeping ? What ails thee that thou
    shouldst weep ?
What shouldst thou grieve for, now that thou art
    found ?
Thy father thou need'st not fear.

Fierce though he seem, to thee
Thou knowest that he is kind.
Then laugh once more and be gay :
Ere thou didst steal away, here in the wild woods
Did we not laugh, were we not gay together ?
Or art thou grieving for yonder slain doe ?
Was she thy playmate ? A sister didst thou deem
    her ?
Or did she give thee suck ? As a mother didst
    thou love her ?
And now dost weep as though
In very deed thy mother here lay slain,
By his hand slain who madly slew her brothers ?
Angels my fury deemed them ; yet too well
Whom I had slain might I surmise thereafter.
What if here too it so hath been,
And once more it hath pleased Him o'er my eyes
To cast delusion, to snare and mock my soul,
That so what most I loved I might destroy !
O my soul, is it possible ?
With Him all is possible.

O Death, Death !
In thee, thee only will I put my trust :
Of thee will I think no ill, nor deem, as those
That hate thee may, that thou with living death

Wilt mock my faith. No, no, thou art
A lord mighty and just, nor wilt reject
Thine own. Am I not thine? Out of thy
    dark
And silent kingdom I came forth, and thither
Would now return. There would I be at rest :
There, there would I shake off
These bonds of life and fate,
This being's shame and misery,
This vain, ceaseless, intolerable strife
Against delusion, madness and despair.

> [*He remains standing awhile with his eyes
> fixed on the ground in moody silence.
> HERZELOIDA re-enters from the right,
> near the place where the doe has fallen,
> and, seeing FRIMUTEL, stands still. A
> moment later FRIMUTEL lifts his head
> and perceives her.*

There ! There ! Oh, it is she ! Nay,
It is her spirit !
There from the slain blood risen, Ah pale, death-
    pale !
Oh misery ! to reproach me art thou come ?
Or in amazement wouldst more surely learn
If, verily, I that have loved thee so
Am he that murdered thee ?

HERZELOIDA

Oh, it is I indeed !   See, Frimutel !
I live, I move !   Shrink not before me thus !
Nay, Frimutel, let not strange thoughts rise
To trouble so thy heart !   Oh, shrink not from me,
From me, no spirit, but thine own dear love.

FRIMUTEL

Stay !   Touch me not now !
If thou indeed dost live, then touch me not.
When thou hast heard what now I am, whom
    once
To love was thy delight, but now thy misery ;
When thou shalt know—

HERZELOIDA

        Nay, hear me, Frimutel !

FRIMUTEL

When all is told, then curse me, and go hence :
Depart and leave me here that I may die.

HERZELOIDA

Oh, hear me speak !

FRIMUTEL

        Heaven's curse, that have I borne,
And still awhile might bear : but thine—
Beneath thy curse how could I still live on ?
Why dost thou weep ?   Shed no tear for me.
Pity not one for whom Heaven hath no pity,
Lest thee too wrath oppress.

HERZELOIDA

                For me fear nothing.
Save for thyself and for our child, in me
Fear now is like a thing outlived, forgotten.
Suffer me here beside thee to remain.
How should I, who alone have caused thy misery,
Not share it with thee ?   Ah, what could I less ?

FRIMUTEL

Is it possible ?   What now I am become,
Canst thou still love ?

HERZELOIDA

        How could I not love thee ?

FRIMUTEL

Thy brothers' blood canst thou forget ?

HERZELOIDA

Alas !

Mine own, no less than thine, must be that guilt.
Oh turn not from me : lift thine eyes to mine,
And they shall teach thee hope.

FRIMUTEL

For me there is

No hope.   But half-fulfilled is now my doom :
Worse yet remains to come.

HERZELOIDA

Listen, Frimutel !

That doom which Kundry by the Grail's constraint
Hath spoken, I too from her own lips know,
And needs must dread no less than thou : yet not
For that will I despair, nor deem that mercy,
Here upon earth of all things most divine,
Of Heaven's justice there can make no part.

FRIMUTEL

For me no more can there be mercy now.

HERZELOIDA

Yes, Frimutel, yes, even now there may.

Even now thou mayst repent, and for thy sin
Find pardon still.

                        Whereof should I repent ?
For what seek pardon ? and from whom ?   Can
      that
Which is not just pardon ?   Can he repent
Whose mind is conscious of no guilt ?   Cease
      then,
Nor urge me to repent.   Though Fate indeed
To unjust power be servile, yet not therefore
Could I by feigned submission and remorse
Trade for its favours basely.   Scorn Fate rather :
Soon like a slighted wanton will it smile,
As now on us it doth ; since thou art come,
And at thy coming, as when daylight brings
Relief to one all night by fierce dreams vexed,
Who knew not if he waked or slept, yet hoped
It was but dreaming, and to unbind his eyes
Hath striven vainly, so now thou art come,
And love anew dawns from thine eyes, I wake
As from a sleep, and far away is fading
Doubt, despair, madness, all that I so long
Have dreamed, and now never again shall dream.
Then be not thus cast down.

Were it not better nobly so to hope
Than basely to repent?

HERZELOIDA

Alas, such hopes
Are blind and vain.

FRIMUTEL

How know we that?   Are love
And hope so vain?   Though they be swallowed up
In misery and death, yet 'tis my faith
They are more wise, aye, and less vain than fear.

HERZELOIDA

Though thou shouldst fear nought else, oh yet fear
    sin.

FRIMUTEL

Evil I fear, not sin, if love be sin.

HERZELOIDA

For those that serve the Grail thou knowest 'tis so.

FRIMUTEL

And for that cause did I renounce its service.

HERZELOIDA

Yet to that holy service dedicated
And separate from thy birth, how then couldst
    thou
Save to thy ruin thus at will renounce
The covenant of thy race, the debt and law
Of thy great heritage?

FRIMUTEL

               Than such a heritage
More dear to me is freedom, and thy love.
So these are mine, then let me welcome ruin.

HERZELOIDA

Ah, Frimutel, thine still while yet I live
Must be my love. But, oh, boast not thy
    freedom.
Insensibly, invisibly around
Both thine and thee the cords of fate are drawn.

FRIMUTEL

What he sees not nor can see, save as thought's

Vain idol, fear's dark dream, no man need dread.

> [*He turns away from* HERZELOIDA *to the child.* KUNDRY *enters from beneath the trees to the left, and during the next few minutes remains standing behind* FRIMUTEL *and* HERZELOIDA *who have not perceived her approach.*

But thou, child of rebellion, thou first-born
Of hope and freedom, would that before I die
I might behold the glory of thy day.
Yet may thine be not such as mine hath been :
And oh may never reckless lust of praise
Tempt thee in pride and ignorance to seek
That evil heritage of shame wherefrom
By me thou hast been delivered at such cost.
No, not for thee such servitude : for that
May thy heart be too noble and too wise.
Not in kings' palaces mid slaves and priests,
Whose wisdom is to fear both God and man—
Not there, my son, an eaglet mid base crows,
Must thou be taught what I would have thee learn ;
Not thus shalt thou be reared : but the free wind,
Snows, frosts, the sunlight and the clouds,
All strong and tameless things of earth and sky
That own no lord, whether as in fierce sport
Contending, or like lovers reconciled,

If so they list, together gently meeting—
These shall thy friends be, from these mayst thou
    learn
That high and fearless wisdom that shall most
Beseem thy birth : then, when thy time is come,
So thou art worthy, slay me, or in disdain
To be the thrall of unjust fate, forbear.
But thee how should I slay ?
Thou art not of the Grail : no part in thee
Shall it usurp, nor in thy glory share.
Truth shalt thou serve, not falsehood ; for mankind,
Not for that Heaven which man's own sick fears
And self-contempt have dreamed, shalt thou endure
And dare, aye, greater things than I have done.

HERZELOIDA

Ah no, no, Frimutel ; not so !
Deadly indeed thine error, and thou lost,
Lost beyond grace, if thou persist therein.
    [*She turns to the infant, and, taking it up in*
        her arms, continues.
O child, child ! Would that to me now
To know thy fate were given !
Yet this I know, let me not doubt this,
That night and day beneath the Grail's keeping
Safe ever shalt thou rest, till, O my child, in thee

103

Shall be revealed its glory.
And in that glory, as in day the night,
Shall this dark night of sin and misery
Fade and become as though it had not been.
Let this faith give me strength still to endure
All else that for thy sake must be endured.

> [KUNDRY *advances a few steps towards them.*
> HERZELOIDA, *on perceiving her, comes*
> *forward with eager gladness to greet her,*
> *while* FRIMUTEL *stares upon* KUNDRY
> *in angry silence.*

Kundry!   Oh joy unhoped!
How, by what chance, couldst thou escape their
    hands?

KUNDRY

So their faith fail not, no wrong need they fear
.That serve the Grail.   Vain were their bonds to
    stay me.
Now hither am I come to bring thee help
And comfort in thy need.   Be of good courage:
For this day must thou follow me far hence
Unto that place appointed for thy rest,
Where thou in peace and holiness shalt rear
This thy son Parsival, till all thy part
In him at length be without blame accomplished,
And at thy hands the Grail receive him back.

According to thy will be my desire.
Ever upon thy wisdom rests my trust.

And yet—what is this I would do !—Not thus—
O Frimutel, I cannot leave thee thus,
Desolate, outcast, beneath Heaven's curse
Unpardoned yet and lost.   Here will I stay,
Here still beside thee ; haply so my love,
And all for love's sake I have borne, misery,
Shame, whereof yet thou know'st not—oh when
     these
Shall move thy heart with pity even to tears,
May then at length repentance, like the sun
Touching the weeping clouds with sudden light,
Shine in upon the darkness of thy soul,
That seeing thou mayst then confess thy sin.
Oh turn not from me thus ! Even in this hour,
Thy last perchance of grace—even now from death
Turn, turn to behold truth's light and live.

[FRIMUTEL remains silent.

KUNDRY (after a short pause)

Thou canst not move him.   All is vain.   Come,
Let us be going.

HERZELOIDA

    Ah no, Kundry, not yet !
How can I so forsake him ! What else now
Except my love is left him ? It may be,
If I stay here, in time his heart will change :
If not, here let me die.

KUNDRY

     What wouldst thou do ?
Not in such wise can Parsival be reared.

HERZELOIDA

Is it come to this ! Is no help left, no hope ?
Must we indeed part thus ? Frimutel,
One word even now, speak but one word of hope ;
Then, be it but hope's shadow, here beside thee,
Till it be.grown to substance, will I stay.

FRIMUTEL

That word I cannot speak.
My hopes are thine no more.

HERZELOIDA

Alas, then, farewell !
Farewell for ever, Frimutel !

FRIMUTEL (*passionately*)

Ah no, no! I cannot let thee go.
Herzeloida, wilt thou thus forsake me?
Out of the pit of terror,
Out of the mists of madness,
Out of the darkness of the shadow of Hell,
Thy love and pity hath delivered my soul
And drawn it forth into the light of day—
For a moment, but a moment, and no more?
And wilt thou thrust me back
To a hell more deep,
To a darkness more terrible,
With mind unclouded now, seeing all things clear,
Yet nowhere seeing hope? Without thee now
Greater than I can bear must be my misery.

> [HERZELOIDA, *deeply moved, remains for a
> while as though in doubt.* KUNDRY
> *speaks no word, yet seems as it were by
> her very presence to impart resolution to*
> HERZELOIDA, *who at length answers.*

HERZELOIDA

It must not be, Frimutel.
Nought but my love, nought but my heart's love
Is mine to give thee now.

My life, too, gladly, how gladly, would I give!
But that to thee I dare not, not to thee.
Broken is now the cup whereof we drank,
And we shall drink no more. Joys did we sow,
And sorrows have we reaped. Love to our feast
We summoned, and behold in Love's place Sin
And Death are set! These soon shall bid us
     rise—
Then torchless through the night. Yet, ere I
     die,
For me is left one service still to do,
About which now I go. For 'tis my faith
That verily the Grail hath chosen our son,
And that in the house of Titurel once more
Monsalvat shall be blessed. Then though he
     slay
Thee whom my soul most loves, though I live
     not
To behold his glory's dawn, yet that alone
Shall give a worth and meaning to our lives,
Which else were nought at all but very vanity,
Dreams only and madness, by sin woven
To be destruction's spoil. But now, I trust,
Through him not altogether shall we die.
O Frimutel, farewell!
For ever and for ever fare thee well!

FRIMUTEL (*calmly*)

Farewell, Herzeloida !
Since so thy faith constrains thee, go, go freely.
Noble is thy heart : little hast thou deserved
Such woe as I have brought thee. Now may
    peace
And happiness at length be thine, whilst thou
To manhood worthily shall rear thy son.
Thereafter—but no more ! So then be it.
For ever fare thee well !
Thou too, my child, farewell !—but not for ever !
      [KUNDRY *goes out to the left, followed by*
           HERZELOIDA, *who bears the child in her*
           arms. Left alone, FRIMUTEL *remains*
           silent for a time, then speaks musingly.
No, not for ever. Till then, O my heart,
Endure. Is it not well ? Have I not too
My faith ? Then for despair what need is mine ?
Thou son of my rebellion,
Though far thou must be severed from me now,
Mine still shalt thou remain. Slave to the Grail
In nowise canst thou be : I fear not that.
Enough from mine thy nature shall inherit.
Yet haply for a season shalt thou serve
Freely, as I too once, till thou that service,

Shalt in thy turn abjure, once more proved vile.
When that day comes, all that so ill hath been,
All that yet must be, shall become most well.
Nay, so it come, what matter though perchance
Alone through my destruction it draw near.

THE END

Printed by BALLANTVNR, HANSON & Co.
Edinburgh & London

Lightning Source UK Ltd.
Milton Keynes UK
UKHW020934300721
387978UK00006B/1170